The Girls
in the
Last Seat
Waving

# The Girls
# in the
# Last Seat
# Waving

MAUREEN McCARTHY

HARBOUR PUBLISHING

Published by
HARBOUR PUBLISHING
P.O. Box 219, Madeira Park, BC V0N 2H0

Printed & bound in Canada


Cover design and photograph by Fiona MacGregor

Some of these poems have appeared in *Event* and *Last Repository*.


CANADIAN CATALOGUING IN PUBLICATION DATA

McCarthy, Maureen, 1944–
    The girls in the last seat waving


    Poems.
    ISBN 1-55017-000-7

    I. Title.
PS8575.C58G5 1989    C811'.54    C89-091003-0
PR9199.3.M417G5 1989

*Dedicated to my mother Anna,*
*and to the memory of my father*

# Contents

## MR. COIN

The house stands there, cracking like a shell
dust roars around it, cars screech to halts, become entangled
disrupt the pulse, hots nights drench the room, the legs jerk
                                              with restlessness
my sister leans out of the window, becomes elongated
resembling an aria in flight
Mr. Coin, non-committal, silent, walks his dog
is it the secret formula of summer that occupies his mind?

His dog sniffs the grass, sausage legs tremble
a bond joins them as they totter on the brink of evening
the routines and the office desks have fallen in
he watches as they go
the past faded like a map
all the roads running downward through his heart
and stopping on his tiny square of lawn
a still kingdom, enclosed behind a flowering hedge.

Absolution should leave a scent, perfumelike upon the wrist
so sudden whiffs may ease the heart, let it sink back
against the cushioned lungs.

## DARKNESS

Darkness soft as pale chiffon falls like rain
stops you in the middle of the stairs
uncoils the springs of thought—
feel again those fragrances
that seep from under walls of time
a deepness stirs inside and vanishes
around the bones of day that held you up till 8 p.m.
collapse drains from off the body, seeps into the grass, a puddle
glistening around your feet, murmuring to itself
of the actions of your arms—the vowels of your mouth
what have you to say, or are you just dragging your carcass through?
darkness swishes through all obstacles
the wind a mix of here and there
tenants stir inside body, one is a child fidgeting
lateness comes and goes, a state of mind
autumn passes through.

## YOUR NAME

Your name squirms
tries to edge through the closed leaves of your life
as it lies untitled, like an unfinished book
abandoned on the desk, beside the globe, the bills
old magazines
feel the shouts within your body calling back and forth
from one region to the other
you have to build your muscles up to handle it
do push ups—sit ups
harden your mind against insurgents
who remember how loneliness used to ooze out of radios
and slide around the room, settling in the lamps
staring down at old men with skinny legs
who slipped notebooks from bedside drawers
wrote poetry
the words crouching down in inner fields, disobedient
full of grievances and mockery, twigs of inexperience sticking
                                              to their clothing.

White curtains sway
ambulances scream down roadways
the injured gasping, images of loss tattooed to their eyelids
children rush from school seats toward the sound
the grass grows quiet, the sky vanishes
is off somewhere rearranging its distant constellations.

## THE MIND

The mind feels stale
banal thoughts float through the bloodstream
"investigations of a dog," the eye again wanders off the line
time wasted burns—what is it you want
Bonnie does not want to take her medicine
the greasy hair sticks up, she must go home to see her son
"Norbert should not have brought me here," the hearing aid is lost
the sky is vanishing, the medicine is spilt.

Is it raining now in Purgatory, are all the semi-sinners huddling
    together?
have they escaped ambition, the rush to Paradise
do they lie down in the shallows, exactly at that point
where the land becomes the sea, where reality fuses with fantasy
sing cowboy songs, long years of feeling escaping through the chorus
leaving them cleansed like newborns in milky nurseries
their hearts poppy red, ungrooved?

## FORMAL PHOTOGRAPH

Petals fall from a center of darkness
that droops upon its stem—the water aged and clear
there is the sound of people bathing in the depths
careless words running over sentences
into the heat that coats the mind, though the blinds are drawn.

I recall someone in a black suit, white cuffs showing
a bridge behind, leading to a place unseen
autos with smoke stalks
puff flowers into the clearest of spring days
brilliant greens, pinks and reds
lift their heads and run into the world
leaving no foot prints, so you cannot see
when you awaken, where they came from, where they went
and yet their scent has rolled into your chest
and lingers like a lion, golden in the desert night.

## WHAT TO SAY

What to say to fathers trailing crazy sons
the father with clenched fists, shards of anger sticking to his suit
the son with saliva trickling down his chin
his mind oozing into openings that appear suddenly in walls.

Don't get drawn in, float like the duck the children painted
orange wings trilling on a yellow body
unwind the colours from their meaning,
let them fall into a heap.

Sip the raw spirit slowly, it will shine inside you
when you stand at the end of day
and brush your teeth, turn out the light
peek out at the neighbour boys swinging lanterns
underneath the hoods of beat-up cars.

Night steals in on them, its cloak full of stars and currents
and a bullfrog bellowing, "I'm here, I'm here,"
sidewalks squiggle off, the wind comes forward
stands before you, frivolous, uncaring
laughs you down, sucks you in

In the morning you will be spewed out
find yourself at the table, eating cereal, darkness rolling back
behind the orbit of your eyes.

# ANNA

Hours gather in the vestibule, eject their scent
deep into the center of the flesh—
like certain snakes they do not move
obtain their prey from what goes passing by.
The poisoned body falls toward the end of summer
the taste of blackberries on its fingertips
sun lost inside its skin—
early darknesses arrive, stiff gardens.

Anna sits on a pile of wood and smokes beside the dahlias
the air shifts temperature, eyes of animals appear
conversations come to life—appear in lighted windows
secret powers, sensual and lonely, wander in the mind
go unnoticed, like old women who know their phones are tapped
who carry on, boiling eggs for lunch
kerchiefs tied underneath their chins.

A wind arises, unties all the houses
they drift into the sky, mingle with the stars
there is grandma's place, roses trailing from its underside
grandpa, drunk and singing on the porch
the moon trying to climb in the window
the cat meowing for his milk.

## EXILES

Long exiles from beginning places
curl and droop around the neck
the feet going all which way
knocking into buildings, sliding down tiled corridors
crashing into pictures strung along the wall
the faces of success, the eyes glancing suspiciously at one another
the shoulders hunched, as if waiting for the knife
waiting to be tipped askew
faint cries echo, rise to ceilings
seep into doors left ajar—darkened rooms
where people sit alone, stare out of windows
at seasons fleeing toward horizons—birds on telegraph wires
days drown in fog
float like water lilies—drift away.

I try always to return—my ticket crumbled in my hand
the train flying through the countryside
rocking on its rails
refusing to make a stop
the conductor, like a beast chained to a wall, growls
                                        and paces back and forth
the doors are placed at dangerous angles.

# SAILING

We sailed on the backs of words into our being
lazed around the uncertain center
Now a wind growls, sheds the darkness, the early morning
blurry sounds seep through the ears
virgin hours float above the head
cast accusing shadows.

The weeks are slipping into spring
they are sneaking out their arsenals
their disregard for quiet slow manoeuvres.

You'll turn around to find the parks are full
the afternoons ablaze, the tulips full of references
You will feel the need to make arrangements
to remove yourself from the nervous edge of deep dreamless sleeps.

## WINTER

Winter moves about the Atlas
crows watch from tree tops
train yards rattle.
The locomotives are exhausted
they have gone from East to West, North to South
searched all the routes
stars press their eyes against the darkness
as if waiting for their father to come home
for that sound upon the step that means the day is done.

Is he somewhere reading on the bus, lost in other people's wanderings
a watch full of moments swishing silently upon his wrist?

Have you seen them, travellers arriving home?
Shaking snow off their boots, hanging up their puzzlement
then sitting down to tea
aloneness, like a simple animal, drifting back into its hiding place.

## ROBINSON

Wednesday arrived, the highways froze
Robinson slept inside his craziness
snug and in no hurry to return
to Vancouver streets, boarding houses, old copies of the *Reader's
Digest*
he hibernates like the earth in winter with all its broken branches
wrapped around its body
the heart marked with an X—just so you know the spot
roots fall across his face
memories like strays, drift away.

Nurses stand in doorways, holler
drink your soup, take your medication
sit out upon the rooftop of your days, your muddled house below
breezes may sprout plantlike from your wrists
pull you upwards, connecting you to bird's eye views
of visitors who even now wait at bus stops
glance at their watches, think of you
the tops of houses, delicate and toylike to your gaze.

## GRAPES

Fat translucent grapes
absorb the fitful sun
their subtle skins full of merriment
Silence lies hidden
emerges, yawning, around 2 or 3
and then there is a banging at the door
children fighting
sheets being thrown into waste baskets
The watch ticks, conceited in its golden case
old men in pale trousers drift down the street.

Think of the inwardness that flashes out in gesture
laziness uprooted, earth smeared on the pant leg
the bloom of sunset dying like a painting that remained unviewed
lost inside the closet with the boots
you can hear the subjects weeping
a flood of wailing fills the room.

There is a wanting to be seen
to be loved
the grass, like wild hair, is strewn with leaves
they fell one by one
and curled into a dreamy brown decline.

## DEAD TIME

Dead time taps anvil-like against the brain
the streets are brown and endless
the white berries grimy
the clock will not be rushed, is rigid in its monotonous approach
leaves sit atop bare branches
upturned, drinking their last rain
dead time—dead time.

I lie like stone in bed
cannot turn toward you
but tender feelings sprout continuously like shoots
cadenzas in the margins seep into the middle
slowly roll like great powers on their flower feet
fill the hallways with the smell of spring—
balls of light lie hidden in the corners
give off mischievous glimmers to ones who scurry down
abstracted, lists scrunched in their hands
searching in the tangled cupboard for shoes full of steps
                                        to carry them away
leaving only the click of heels on sidewalks
grains of sand like meteors, sparkling underfoot.

## MORNING

Morning, the vanishing of dreams—
where do they go?
Do they sink back into the brain
sleep and wait for us to re-appear?

The day is packed with surgeons in disguises
the ankles tense, the heart in spasms
words in herds, stalk
"I wish that I had died" she said, as she sat huddled in the tub
her body scarred, her head shaven—

"Lie down and sleep and have no fears."
visions of John Donne advising—
a grey light forms in the aisle, the pews are stony
later, walking in the streets, you wonder where they went, those
    moments
is it nothing can be kept?
what you will become awaits you, a station you will pull into
the rafters filled with pigeons, pools of wind swooping.

The reflection of the sun slides down the window glass
settles and burns out upon the rug
in reveries perhaps she hears, the peal of bathers
wading into water.

## CT SCAN

"It's a matter of shadows," the doctor said, explaining the CT scan
"the tumor could be here, could be there
it's how you tilt your head and where the shadows fall"
a cocoonlike office, a polite smile
can the mind protect if there are sections missing
or will the contents all spill out
the caged autumn mornings, the old car rides longing to continue on
conversations searching for an ending, will they leak out and wander
   off?
The last heaven hides, casts shadows on the brain
feel them fluttering as you wave your hand to say goodbye.

You smile and drum your fingers on the counter
talk of taking buses, what unconscious routes will pull you?
a lone figure standing at the corner
the wind blows westward high above your youth
the night advances
you wait with all your language in you
but it seeps out, strews notes up and down your arm
and here is one your mother wrote
"he is a gentle boy, send him home by nightfall."

## REPORT

"the sensorium was clear," he said
in some are always shadows, rain on elms
think of Kafka and his terrors
his night room full of gnawing rats
jump up and get them with your shoe
while the mountains stare in through the windows
they move toward you, want the place that you are standing in
the air sticky with tuberculosis settles on the plates
fills you with disgust as you feel the world's rim tighten at your waist.

The world can grow so small for tired ladies in pulp towns
the four-wheel drive beside the camper truck.
"the sensorium was clear," he said, except for a few twigs poking up
a squeaky sound that flared when she moved.
They stop at the outer edge of warming rain
examine their finger nails, sigh, get that martyr look
the yellow of forsythia glares
cars circle persistently searching for a parking place
the hall fills, the lecturer will speak on "Intimacy"
an expert flown in, twenty dollars for a ticket.

Our group makes its way around the buildings
the air fills with the sea, the muscles bending into blooms
a statue of King George, rain dripping off his nose, bows
one feels shy before such tender kings.

## LURE

Pages lure the mind
howls perch on crevices, wild flowers
a red moon, the sort that Rousseau liked, lowers itself into Paradise
may not return again—people sleep
their cats circle round them, eyes glassy in the shadows
you can hear them at the bottom of your consciousness breathing
their tails like question marks curl into your images.

The ironing board is folded up, the iron put away.
Wind sweeps the curtains along the floor, the swoosh of complexes
rubbing at each other until the skin peels off, rawness underneath
staccato sounds like sharp pointed leaves rising
divisions leave the dreamer, fight in hallways
plaster heads roll off—splinter into fragments.

Birds inside their covered cages twitter—
in the midnight yard colours deepen, confusion vanishes
cars roll by, their tires humming
all is perfectly arranged in childlike order.

## WANDA

Anxiety crawls from holes along the baseboards
creeps along the hallways, erodes the bones
you must go bandaged, only the eyes showing
and the mouth swollen, needs to breathe
the brain is soggy with information that drips down the skin.

Is it the fear of moving on at all
no possessions with you for protection
sun searing through your eyelids?
where is that false heel packed with subversive directives
that helps you cross the barrier between the day and the idea of day?

Wanda, pull the curtains back, look at that cement next door
the garden down below, the roses growing rosier
through and through the middle of it all
the Northern Star still steady, its shine falling with a tingling sound
like drops of rain onto the center of your head
it splits you open—sews you up
small stitches run like fleeing moments behind each ear.

## NOTHING WORKS

Nothing works at change of seasons
corners of the house collapse—the sky invades
Derek refuses to arise
"I'm not a God, I don't want special treatment
but I have to stay in bed and work my problems out
then I'll wash"
the clothes lie like outcasts in a heap
the guitar underneath the desk eats through the floor
music hidden in its cheeks
darkness gathers in the room, drips into the core of plants
Derek hides inside a mound of Derek bones
twigs of hair stick out, a blossom eye
the door narrows
soon the bed will not fit through
will get lodged sideways, the mattress springs tightening
around his ankles
while worlds plunge by—buses leave for town
his heart beat like a slow drum all through winter
waiting—waiting—waiting
we heard it in the office as we plotted our escape
our faces pale, our mouths set.

## CATS

Cats waiting to be fed sit solemnly in doorways
the table stumbles through the meal—the candles laugh
the children leaning into summer, movies on their shirt-tails
lampoon the loon, its diver's cry.

Lakes invaded draw in their thoughts
grow mute, sneak under land
inward to apartment basements, bubble up around the laundromats
their scent clings now to your shirt.

You stand looking in the mirror, your brow raised
sun, like a power, streaming through the window
a frog leaps from your pocket
streams fed by jets of light and dark
sprout out your orifices, rise round you like a prayer.

# NEURONS

The neurons in a tangle pulsate into the ears
dangle, scream at the cold
the tips of trees cry out
their wailing gathers in the clouds, turns them mauve
we will have rain again tonight
it falls like eyelids over eyes
blows out the outer world, as if it were a candle
a skinny man lopes across the street
hesitates, does not know which way to turn
does he see the streets running from him
the seasons twittering on twigs and vanishing
sleepless words searching for a form
they hunt through factories, apartment corridors
see images in drifts, but disjointed, lacking wholeness
bus stops stay put, rub their feet together, lack imagination
watch people getting off at wrong places
or is it anywhere will do for the shy and schizophrenic
Owen sits a long time over coffee, he is adjusted to the uneventful life
reads unheard of books, has had enough of heroes
rests his long frame, cowlike on the grass
gazes up at the moon, meets its eye looking back at him.

## TUGGING TIDE

The bed, waiting like a tugging tide
gnaws around the ankles
darkness flattens all the houses
the mind strays into winter
to the way your father looked smoking by the bedroom light
lemon counter tops—the heater humming on.

The throat is full of stale words marching out in suburban order
it is the lungs where feelings hide
the little alveoli crammed with mild rebellion—
they crowd around the esophagus, taunt it with recriminations.

Celestial equators turn silently around us
plants exude the smell of love
the air grows soft at evening time
drips like water colours down the passage ways
the slender light moves back and forth between the decades
does not wish to settle.

# PIANO MUSIC

You are practising three blind mice with chords
ten o'clock waits for the minutes to arrive
the first coolness of the day descends
the street looks different as if composed of shadows
the sound of a motorcycle, where is he rushing to
in upstairs rooms everywhere old people are trying to get to sleep
their hearts like wells grown deep and moving toward the center
the coolness wraps around their legs, rubs their arches
think of long races over arctic snows, dog sleds sliding through the
   night
ice covering the lakes, fish in streaks of red and gold throbbing like a
   beat

the earth pulls inward, the air palpable with stories
they flutter on unseen wings, the head turns toward the sound
the body journeys onward, while the mind dallies in vanished rooms
gets caught in half remembered rhymes
are you too nostalgic for that time you felt completely loved?
acts of devotion flare
the wind rushes like a lonely man
across the fields and through the darkness that descends, an iron lid.

## THE DAY

It's hard to be precise about the day
the different rains
the words with soft tongues licking your stiff arms
the sound of rustling in another room.

Why need reassurance ask the flowers
they are crammed into a vase
a mess of ragamuffin pinks resembling storms at sea
a scent hints at bliss
it wafts its way past thought and joins vast forces
already long in motion.

Sometimes I want to talk
but she keeps writing out her shopping list
coffee, soap, etc. etc. her being, hidden in a forest of past years,
runs in and out
dogwoods stand outside her kitchen window, their creamy blossoms
    purring
does she float with lonely ease in private rooms
feel someone smiling in her?

## QUEENSBOROUGH BRIDGE

Goya drew upon the walls—have you seen those figures
did they stare and stare—begin to follow you around
lean beside you over railings
as you watched the sun go down behind the railroad tracks.
They keep gesturing and drooling
sometimes they disappear only to be spotted once again
along that seam that connects the body to the soul
it is invisible, though you can see it in the eyes, the mouth
hours drop one by one
a bird gathers bits of twine, flies away, returns
warm air hangs above the house, descends at night
moves unobtrusively like an old woman in a country town
the river silently asleep or is it waiting
see the face immersed in water, one hand ploughing in above the head
the other coming out beside the hip
what watery thoughts are being born in that water body
what wisps of pleasure tingling the spine
green waves like puffs of breath pass through her skin
fish nestle in her ear, think of flight and of pursuit
the wider world, the private universe, fatigue.

## ROLLING STREETS

We drive the rolling streets
past hours that stand in line like rows of houses
ambiguous and silent
once they were real—moved their airy limbs
timidity devours me—a brooding type of mind
we are so deeply what we are
we cannot shift the slightest bit—someone said it
I read them all—stuff them in my marrow
sun floods the lawn, a truck's engine idles in the lane
the cat licks his paws, his eyes shut in ecstasy
does he dream of brothels
lost girls soft and fine, lingering on boardwalks
nights fall from the sky
layer upon layer—a gauzy substance like a sheet upon us
I feel your heart beating in your chest
                              fast and light.

## THE YARD

The yard is still
except for swallows who twirl and zig-zag through the dimming air
she advances toward the walk
one hand moves constantly inside the other
"a family trait," her words trail off like dry leaves across a winter
    garden
the earth shifts
shakes the unprepared, the ones with loose footing
there was a time when she would go up on the roof
to shovel off the snow
she strode lightly there as if she were in Eden
the snow tumbled down, a sleeping sound
the night is clear, the wind plays with our clothing
what will be the true prayer at last
the one that asks for nothing?

## DO YOU FEEL

Do you feel sometimes against your body the thud of something lost?
a way of thinking gone, sunk into a distant corner of the brain
with a patch of street, melting snow
the stem that whirled out to your destiny—
bend down the oars, feel the pressure of the water
the boat moves forward silently through turning tunnels
the thoughts that hold the neck erect slacken, the chin falls upon
                                        the chest.


The night rushes by
a man weeps, his dentures out, his cheeks sucked in
we sit by the door where there is a little light, read
give him a cigarette, one per hour
do not let him bang his head against the wall
"a starry night" by Van Gogh, have you seen it?
the charged movements of the stars
the village sleeping far below like a time of innocence snuggling down
days fall from the years, settle on the lawn
the flowers watch, still centered, they have retained their principle
                                        of beauty.

# TINTAGEL

The seagulls cried all night
the wind left rhymes about the door
we lay in bed, felt the closeness—and the far away
journeying
my self feels lost—my skin looks strange
we came upon a church on cliffs above the sea
a rash of graves, a musty smell of age
Tintagel—where worlds have come and gone
we said some prayers there
though I do not believe
they must still be there
they will have grown old, grown tall
perhaps at night they wander in that unfamiliar land
search endless streets for us
make sounds like leaves that lie upon the pavement.

## A LUMINOUS BLUE

A luminous blue falls over the rim of the earth and drips into the
     milky way
white blossoms with no themes glide through fantasy and day
Tom, goiter-eyed and hamsterlike burrows down the corridor
for many years demented, and he does not wash, a streak of mustard
     yellow
tightly sprung
the walls stand back, grow pale, his room shakes
the shame of not loving the unlovable stands like a cave before one
have you knocked into it? got lumps upon your forehead
or did they sprout inside your heart, nodules rubbing in the lower
     chamber

the evening spreads away again, have you been left in parking lots
a little lost as to your course, wondering if the building
will collapse, the pavement melt beneath your feet
what does this landscape mirror? is it foreign to your mind
or have you been a traveller? the ways we learn are sideways moving
crablike—the legs out around it—crawling crookedly
toward pools, the smell of shorelines
clinging to the underside of rocks, as if to the deeper things
one should never let escape.

## FOR AUGIE

No one wants to enter
I too dislike her, she rolls from side to side
like an argument in a narrow bed
the voice crashes on the window glass, "I don't
    want that"
enormity lurks beneath the bureau
swirls out and swallows her now and then
spits her back to the smell of urine in the sheets.
Who will find the food to feed the dying?
the Reverend, like a reed, wavers in the corridor
a darkened corridor, it should have winds like windy shores do
to blow across the brow, the sound of waves searching for a resting
    place

at night, at times boundaries loosen
one wanders in another's mind, hears the intermittent sound of rivers
    running
cries of deep ambition, pride
then the dying have some food for us
we stand awkwardly, feel a surge of gratitude
it is better than imagination, these meetings immediate and real
without warning the pointed face snaps shut, locks with a shrill whine.
We turn out the hall lights at ten, turn on the office radio
sit out on the roof and watch the water lapping round the windows
tell tall tales and even kiss.

## ENCOUNTERS

Can one dive and escape like Houdini
through all the regions of the mind
the arms like eggbeaters whirling in the seaweed
the heart nibbling on foreign languages

Faces twitch in absent-minded exertion
the repositories of dreams that melt as they retreat
my thoughts fly off—colliding as they go
while the odour of mild winter afternoons stirs the old brain
that lies beneath the new
causing it to raise its sleepy head, cast its eyes toward windows

The speaker stands, droops like limp celery
clears her milky throat, begins
words drift like soapy bubbles—pop quietly and splutter
surges of annoyance jet through endless information
listeners glance away.

Do they wonder what will matter in the end?
everything is moving—pacing round in circles
that curve into the road and join the endless journey of the sky.

I drowned at end of day
sank into the company of strange and brilliant fishes
she was down there too
alone like me and shouting "Look—look!"

## MORNING SKIES

Morning skies, bushes streaked with rust
bits of snow dotted on the ground
the trees locked in frost wait for an escape
a wind to rattle at their bars, words of comfort
whispered from the earth
no one comes—but passing eyes observe
how the details of the universe move in their own rhythm
how birds burst from skinny trees
and small actions give birth to wild passions

the nurse tidied up the room, removed the perfume, the letters
veined with voices speaking of the unseen
low lamps—radios playing Stardust
she was fat, got her bum stuck in the doorway
irrationality rebelled behind her, pelted her with objects she had
                                                    tucked away
let her go—pull down the blinds—don't get out of bed again
burrow into visions, whatever seems absurd,
you will need a friend to bring you food, deliver messages
grow strong slowly, emerge, your suitcase packed with odds and ends
                                                    lusty cries.

## POEM FOR MY DAUGHTER

The sky gone dark with passion, the clouds with their arms touching
the fire licks its power
life grows in disarray
spins silently from out of us creations which we wear
sometimes against our will.
Some would like to draw their hands across your face, feel your skin
it is propriety that keeps them still
does not allow their eyes to linger
I wonder will you wake up slowly or like some flowers all at once
houses drift in the night, trees wear stars
streets, old and narrow wind around the stores
like a sentence in a book that just goes on and on
not making any sense, but lovely
stray sometimes, in your red dress, blue stockings
along the margins, kick loose the mysteries there.

## ELSA

The fire hisses like a cat, the cat sleeps and grandma too
and all the five star generals
they lie naked now between the sheets
their limbs like tendrils from a gentler time
the earth dips, loaded down with bomber planes
think of you and I called out to stand shoulder to shoulder
waiting for our turn
panic racing through the senses, dogs barking
we sit askew inside the cup of night, the moon upon the rim
landscapes hide beneath the hedges, eat the darkness
grow fat, bulge with irresistibilities
sometimes in the early morning you find yourself inside one
emerge dazed, bread inside your pockets
but there is the lawn waiting to be crossed
islands of red poppies showing through, apple trees with revelations
they will not be fooled into declaring—
they will leave them locked inside your brain, for you to free
the world intrudes, impales your concentration
Elsa spends hours scrutinizing the papers
she stands endlessly beneath the one bright light
you can see her eyes trying to figure out which one you are
the edges of your face are blurred, the walls have vanished
she feels the ground giving way
hangs on to the counter, argues politics
passion burns her like a fire.

## A CHILLY AIR

A chilly air, it rises as you speak of winter
you running down a darkened street behind a friend
what bad thing had you done?
do you believe in evil—hear its heavy legs behind you?
turn quickly, nothing there but Kiwanis pool
a few children on inner tubes playing in the mist
but fears infiltrate, jealousies, betrayals
they sit like ugly relatives wearing gaudy clothes, red rouge
yet they have their soft side too, try to bribe you with insecurities
squeeze against you in the hallway
hold out a fleshy cheek waiting for a kiss
do you remember pulling back, sneaking out the door?

"In my father's mansion are many rooms,"
think of one bright hall leading to another, freshness
the awkwardness of being human stirs tenderly around one
he hid all day beneath his blankets, the door closed
his lunch grew cold and soggy, distances yawned before his feet,
    deepened
his brother, looking stranded, wandered amidst the endless plains of
    wall
outside, late summer spreads its wings, lifts you as if you were a kite.

## IT WILL COME

It will come, a raging wind that tears across your mind
uproots language, leaves a howling
the blinds neither up nor down
the hours held at bay, released too slowly to crawl in voids
perhaps there will be someone checking on you
"is everything okay?" what does that mean?
but we out distance all the words, the categories
Mignon in her search for bus fare, arms to fold about her
her love scattered like the fluff of dandelions
walked delicately to the mental hospital
as easy thoughts screamed through the grillwork of spring trees
the sun burned on brick walls
we sat out in chairs, clasping bits of power to our breasts
glad it was not us

everything eludes the thing it's wrapped in
floats slightly out of reach, in air throbbing
with wasted actions, stray emotions, days that hang like blossoms
blow away, leave a scent of pleasure on the leaves
dawn seeps into sleeping rooms
over people shrouded in their dreams
their arms flung out, their masks split open
revealing faces fallen backwards into youth
one feels an invader watching them, almost a thief
shoes scatter when the flashlight lights upon them
the night moves on, insomniacs and assorted others
can hear the humming of its wheels racing over bumpy ground.

## OLD LADY

Leaves hang carelessly upon the branches
little discs of pale green and yellow, a rash of them
a wintry light shot with sombre colour
recalling countries you have imagined, Scotland, the Hebrides
places strung with lanes, people with small divinities percolating in
     them
here an old lady's back yard—twigs tied in bundles
she roams there in her rubber boots, an explorer like Columbus
her patch of earth, a ship, reels around the planet
rests in oceans—drop your hands into the water
the fish sleep, their colours drawn in, wrapped like works of art
inside their hearts
is it unfathomable, what great and tender eyes have seen
do conflicting feelings catch at the opening of their throats
she holds her rake, ever moving things surround her
the house at the far end slumbers, its windows like passages to worlds
soft and full of sofas

# KEATS

Mary has to stop to get her breath, her lungs rattling
with pneumonia and Player's Please
we stand around and wait
cough-cough-cough—it pads on noisy feet the lion cough
Keats died on this day a thousand years ago
the letting go upon him, he stood alone—we stand on Cresbrooke
   Street
beneath a globe of light you can see the branches swaying
the sky gone dark with bruises
Peter limps beside me
he wants to learn to live, he says it every day and smiles politely
outside his window there is a tree escaped from Hardy
it wants to pull him in, soothe his cheeks
but his head bumps against the bottom of his chair, his back collapses

an old lady with a Woodward's bag crammed with Phoenix wings
zigzags like a schoolgirl across the windy field
will she go home—strap them to her back—smile a secret smile
I want to rush somewhere
feel my hat flying off my head, the earth springing against my feet
all the fragments joining.

## MY FACE

My face seen fleetingly in a store mirror
the bony structure sticking out unceremoniously like a gutted house
the eyes grown small and faded as if washed by waves and lying in the
    sand
windy clouds scattered us along
you should know who you are and
what you stand for, she said
the pigeons coo upon the roof, defiant creatures
a bit of sky dangling from their mouths
the sun came out, dogs appeared
and children with their sweaters blowing
the earth sinks down and down, has no bottom
does it matter—these doubts about conviction, philosophy
that one spends one's time leading people into empty rooms
telling them they will be helped by new inventions
while the trees outside bob
the clouds gather into towers, give off sparks of sultry pink
what is that connection between people I often fail to feel
the birth of care you experience when alone
sitting at a table eating soup, glancing at a book
the sky like a diva sinking into lower notes
where does it go when face to face you feel the words escaping, the
    mind stopping
a man fainted in the parking lot
a woman put her purse beneath his head
flapped her arms above his body, talked to him
a taxi driver phoned for an ambulance
like heroes, they took action
even if sometimes they find themselves staring at the earth
knowing it is nothing they can measure.

# LEAVES FLY UP

Leaves fly up, angels with their cargoes of dead soldiers
they leave the squares forlorn
the hospital leans over, heavy with its burden of survivors
one cries out all day, you can hear him as you rush by
and view the pink clouds, the late roses
a clump of alders sway continuously, season after season, fill with
    growth
Wilfred has been studying them, his eyes like hollows tunnelling down
                                     to ocean floors.
You have to go with lanterns there, leave the doctors in their chairs
their minds stuffed with remedies
the sky floats in around him, carries him away
do you think he will be able to return?

Oh Galileo, discover, speak to us about the stars
about those things larger than ourselves
that pull us toward them with light persistent hands
start the car, turn the headlights on
the bushes suddenly illuminated, wavering and delicate
they are bending into shapes, O's and A's
feel their breath upon your brow
the day going down against your body.

## SHADOWS

The shadows of the bees flit against the wooden fence
the leaves move
the flowers and the sunlight
sentences "I was wax between your fingers" swish
swallowlike, circling low above the hungry grass
a fragrance breaks against the mind
the freshness of zigzagging thoughts continually escapes
as one sits at dinner tables, dips into bowls of conversation
deep lakes remembered slide like slips against the skin.

Stars shone with a force that almost frightened
seemed to want to speak with us
warm themselves inside our arms
the fish watched silently, now and then one leapt
deer waited, their lady legs poised.

Pluto drifts around the galaxy
looks out at miles of darkness
curving like forgotten railroad tracks
around the earth's moon and indifferently descending.

## CLARENCE

Leaves chase the branches of the trees, cars careen
blonds wave from the backs of years that have spun away
the lounge grows hot, windows steam
his heaviness like a set of doors slides open
feel that warm breeze breezing through your breast bone
there is the fluttering of birds, the sound of thick despairs
                                        stumbling
Clarence, lost in corridors, his legs collapsing
shuffles to the smack
of juicy leaves as they wrap around his thoughts
all is gone, but one shirt drying on the radiator
and some daffodils, their eyelash petals turned toward him
his day closes over
farewells falling through the cracks
tendrils from a future time poking through the silence.

## STONE COLUMN

A stone column looms within us
packed with birds waiting to take flight
listen, their wings are straining
the air is empty, clear and cold, as if drained of tenderness
the flowers wait to call farewell
their small mouths pursed in readiness
the moon is lonely on his lonely path
do you hear his cry on the inside or the outside of your head
it takes a shape that howl, a colour
falls to the earth, wanders aimlessly about
bumps into us sitting at the picnic table out beneath the trees
the in-laws and the babies stir like a summer breeze
do not see it sitting there between them, a lean loneliness
staring at the potato salad, the baked chicken
if you offer it some wine it will cradle you like a lover in the center
of its eyesight
feel your heart relax, your mind expand
the crowd moves about the lawn, admires the butterflies
that look of pleasure simplifies the face
the front porch settles down into the hollows of the night
the lilac bush folds its branches across its fat lilac chest
does not desire what should only be imagined
praises the blossoms circling its wrists.

## EACH DAY

Each day now the trees grow leafier
the streams fatter
morning seeps through like a goldfish rising to the surface
but still its chilly, bleakness refuses to depart
to float like ice down stream
surrender to the ocean.

We threw leaves into the river
watched their nervous journey until they vanished
like uncles, fathers, aunts met only once
it rained and then the sun came out
I want to fall away from all ideas of striving
flit around, land like a butterfly on irises
shaped and curved and powdered purple
leaning into one another, like a group of women
languorous and chatty.

## LATE MORNING

The sun persists
it is going to meet victory at noon
will not be waylaid, gardens wait.
Old men on porches watch their dogs
they know that it will come.

Shadows die patiently along the wall
they have broken from that great patience that lurks around the
　　woods.
Someone threw a sofa into them, it lies now on its side
like a ship upon the ocean floor
leaves swim around it, its contents are oozing out.

Will they leave it thinner, lighter, able to float
a resting place above the clouds for refugees and tired birds
for cows jumping over the moon
who want to stop and think about it
before returning to their ordinary life, the morning milking
　　　　　　　　　　　　　the midnight plaintive mooing.

## STRUTS

He struts toward us
doused in beer and business talk
slickness dripping from his elbows
his ears—are they closed to sound
or do words trickle through
innocent adjectives and nouns sliding down and fainting
in the airless voids, beads of feeling covering their brow?

Motorcycles speed along the freeway
their fumes terrorize the air
daisies wilt as they go by
but the streams keep gurgling
caterpillars crawl under lily pads
morning is filled with ditches
where one can lie, hidden by sweet smelling grass
a rainbow green
silence, like a diviner, poking overhead.

## THE STRINGS OF LIFE

The strings of life lift the shoulders up
the flesh, like a bodyguard softened by fatigue
folds about the heart.
Did you sleep all weekend
fight the lure of soundless worlds that keep you off your balance?

The sky goes slipping North behind the clouds
while a smile like a hypocrite shuffles in the mouth
Have you been at burials in which the victim rose
returned to mock you
just when you were sighing with relief, pulling down the blinds,
but searches inward are a waste.

I fall in love with other people's words,
like to feel them blowing in the cracks inside my brain
mingling with the ordinary, the everyday
like a river flowing by the freeway.
Three old people stood there, a hat blew off one, fell into the water
the sturdier woman waded in, retrieved it
held it in the air like a prize wrestled from the mystery.

## LEAF

Not a leaf is stirring
sounds rumble through the ground
like worn beliefs thundering home
to where they can fall apart—drift
into different rooms—sleep
like tired fathers with lined faces
remote—their thoughts forever elsewhere
a winter light wanders down the hallways.

Tiny fish flash like bits of turning silver
aerial and carefree in living room aquariums
a red dial glows inside the radio
its faucet lips murmuring of Coca-Cola.

I put on felt slippers, pull a blanket up
lie upon the couch—the clock has stopped
nothing can advance—change position
all expectations cease, the drapes stay drawn
only the fish remain awake—zigzag like soundless gossip.

## SCHIZOPHRENIA

Salesladies with pink hair, violet eyes
chatter across the aisles
their voices burst like bubble gum
stick to the lipsticks, perfumes.
The lights forever on wall out the rain
it wanders down the street lashing the pale month
until its pulse becomes audible through the downpour of the leaves
storms follow, the snag of complications
the world collapses
scenes remain, one of youths
the beast of torment curled around their chests.

Together we have watched the sea settle in its bed
the mountains fold their wings
vessels full of quiet glide along the hidden surface
sometimes they ignite, flare in the darkness
illuminate the topography of our being
dissolve like other's lives into our own.

## URGENCY

Urgency runs like a speedy waltz through grass
yet there is no pinnacle that one will reach in 10 months or 10 years
just the musings of the day that come and go
a sense of vertigo.

Boys rock the house next door
it swings around the bar of midnight
foundations crumble, walls fly off, girls scream
sleep rolls up to roof tops
and scans the sea for submarines, for heroes rising from the waves.

One waits and watches
a candle flickers, as if it were a feeble breath
connected to a heartbeat
will the sky kiss it back to life?

An abandoned birch comes into view
its bark is peeling off, there is a paler one beneath
its many selves lie one inside the other
do they whisper back and forth when no one is around?
discuss the single-minded cedars, the pros and cons of inconsistency?

## VOICE BOX

The voice box crammed with words
releases them in spurts
so that they spill or dribble from our mouths
and are soon slain and stuffed inside our pockets

hurry on—down halls, around corners
yes Sir, no Sir
routines rattle in the rooms, behind the doors
put your arms above your head
do you feel their forces pressing on your breast bone?

The day sinks
stillness loiters in the long line of the sky
there are the midnight noises, the squeal of tires, the footfall
                                        of a jogger

in ponds thoughts swim together
sling themselves in lines
a feeling running through them
they swim across the ceiling and down the wall
as if they were a moving light
suddenly they're gone, the room again in darkness
the ticking of the clock.

In the house next door, the TV stays on all night
blurry images move across the window like incidents that cannot rest
until they're understood
will they break away and flee, rattle at the door?
I hear the lock shake in agony.

## THE TEMPESTS

The tempests have stood up
are crowding at the windows, their chaotic eyes burrowing
they want to overtake you—shake you into everyday
think of the malaise of the sleeper who awakes
it lies upon him like an illness, he has no patience
with ordinary interruptions, he is longing to return to old devotions
as hummingbirds in flight across the fields turn
and scurry back to first obsessions
the trees watch, arrange their leaves in ancient patterns
spread their tones over grass and into flickering light
Edens are expanding, statues of Liberty sprout like dandelions
the wind ruffles their high lamps
benches elongate, wait for various behinds
tall tales wander arm in arm, wait to feel knees and hands upon them
it does you good to sit down and watch the buses pass
the slow easing into traffic, the girls in the last seat waving.

**Maureen McCarthy** was born in Montreal in 1944 but has spent most of her adult life in Vancouver, where she works as a nurse. Her first book, *She Reminds Me of Vermeer,* was published by Harbour Publishing in 1980.